The Power & Miracle of Words

Lucky Kaur

Authored by Lucky Kaur

© Lucky Kaur 2021

Cover Design: Marcia M Publishing House Images:

Edited by Marcia M Publishing House Editorial Team, Lee Dickinson

Published by Marcia M Spence of Marcia M Publishing House,

West Bromwich, West Midlands the UNITED KINGDOM B71 1JB

All rights reserved 2021 Marcia M Publishing House.

The author asserts the moral right to be identified as the author of this work. This book is sold subject to the conditions it is not, by way of trade or otherwise, lent, hired out or otherwise circulated in any form of binding or cover other than that in which it is published. No part of this publication may be reproduced, stored in a retrieval system or transmitted in any form or by any means (electronic, mechanical, photocopying, recording or otherwise) without prior written permission from the author or publisher.

www.marciampublishing.com

Table of Contents

About the Author 4

My Unique Yellow 5

Be Yourself – In the World Circle 7

A 'She' and 'He' Tale! 9

Those Memories 11

This Photo of Mine 13

The View From My Window 14

The Fantasy World 16

Why Do I Keep Writing? 17

When the Brain Had a Chat With the Heart! 19

Why Be Too Judgemental? 22

Today the Wardrobe Was Talking to Me 24

A Heart the Secret Place … 26

Eyes 28

Life in a Lockdown! 30

Life After Lockdown 32

Good Time Will Come 33

Nostalgic College 34

Simplicity 36

About the Author

I have immense passion for writing and my favourite style/hobby is poetry.

Poetry is very therapeutic for me and I believe it's an effective way to express ideas. Writing is a very unique and sacred part of my life - as it's a platform where one has the ability to capture and visualise anything in the form of words...

My Unique Yellow

My very special Yellow brings light into dark.
Such a powerful shade it is – the eternal light of spark.

My Yellow is my smile,
My Yellow is my pain.

My unrequited love for Yellow – is beyond words to explain ...

This Yellow divine, is a blessing from almighty.
An expression from the one up there, residing close by.
Nothing can beat the emotion of this Yellow,
nothing can reach so high ...

My Yellow is my devotion,
My Yellow is my trust.
Closer to purity away from dust.
My Yellow is my desire,
My Yellow is my dream.

My Yellow is part of my destiny, a magical glow of gleam.

My Yellow is precious, my Yellow is power.
It's an everlasting fragrance, mesmerising like a flower.
My Yellow is my pride, embellished like a crown.
My Yellow is blissful in the universe town.

Soothing like silver, glowing like gold.
This Yellow is universal – a miracle untold.

I'm the Blue sky, but my Yellow sunshine completes my scene, when we both mix together – we flourish evergreen.

Be Yourself –
In the World Circle

The world is a circle, we are a part of living here.
Our society makes our circle, where we all have a share.

Ones that say, "We are always with you,"
In hard times may disappear.
This circle may be challenging to walk in, so handle yourself with care.
Haters and debaters will all the time appear.
Why lose your own identity for them –
Is it really fair?

Some may agree you're right, others will say you're wrong. End of the day, we all have to make our personal decisions – so continue to be strong.
Perform your part wisely in this circle, keep your foundation firm.
Make an individual movement with grace, inspire someone to learn.

Avoid the attempt to satisfy all the crew out there, rather be truthful to yourself. Don't lose yourself by soaking in the mixture, don't try to be someone else.

You have come alone, so recognise your powers –
Just kindly Be Yourself.

A 'She' and 'He' Tale!

She, the prime creation, she gives and then lives.
Not much does she take, not easy she gets a break.
Continuous and everlasting is her commitment, very unique has nature designed her make!

It's amazing how the 'He' hardly agrees to make any type of compromise – whereas the 'She' is titled the 'Symbol of Sacrifice'!
Usually, she bids farewell to her kin and needs to move on. However, the 'He' does not have that element of separation, in the same house, he can happily carry on …

'She' looks into the mirror every day, quietly with an inner-talk has a lot to say. A powerful personality, she continues to convey.

'She' must surrender and be out of sight – because not very safe for her is to be out in the night. Whereas 'He'

does not get the spark – until he roams through late night, with his mates in the dark!
'He' naturally privileged care-free can consume, managing to attend an urgent 'nature's call' – creeping in a corner out of sight ...
However, 'She' wisely limits her intake, because not so easy will it be for her the 'nature's call' to chase – in a 'rough' public place.

With a convincing, sensitive smile, bravely she appears, secretly hiding behind a thousand tears. She merrily continues to walk, challenging all the fears! Wearing a crown of responsibilities and determination, an angel she appears ...

To live this 'She' it takes a lot, because she has always given a lot more than she's got.
The 'He' is bold but the 'She' can sometimes stay untold ...

May flourish the both 'She'-'He' in life that's real.
The 'She' and 'He' is a deep epic tale to experience and feel.

Those Memories

When I look down that memory platform,
very far goes my train.
Shockingly, I think to myself – Yes, it all has become the past now.
That time can never come back again.

That unique spark still enlightens my soul, how can I explain?
But it all does not exist anymore, and none gets the blame.

It all feels very nostalgic, looking back at the past.
But I must agree to the fact – this time moved on very fast.

Very passionate and magical was this journey, very powerful is the memory train. It took me back many stations, beyond words to explain ...

It does not matter if that time has moved forward –
Those memories still exist in my heart.
Those memories are eternal for me, they made the beginning –
the divine start!

This Photo of Mine

Looking back at this photo,
it makes me ask myself –
Is that person really me or is it someone else?

Because that me was enthusiastic,
very colourful and bright.
That me was very shiny, in darkness or light.
That me was dramatic, with dreams and fantasy.

This photo is bringing new desires again,
repeating flashbacks of the past.
This photo makes me question myself, how did it all change so fast?

This photo is admirable, showing the original presence of me.
This photo is my favourite –
a wake-up call to see.

I really miss myself in this photo,
please embrace me once again.
I want to come back and feel like this photo,
I want to live this me again!

The View From My Window ...

Outside my window, what do I see?
A Fantasy world – my vision has created to step in,
waiting for me ...

A picturesque view, that's what I see.
It's much more radical than the "real" world –
That's my guarantee!

I see the sun talking to the clouds:
"I promise, I will shine defiantly, as I am the lamp of grace. I promise my rays of light will be bright enough, to enlighten the whole space and make this world a glorious place."

I see the rain talking to itself:
"The view from this window is far too blissful to steal its glory, with my gloom and blur. Now staying away, I would rather prefer ..."

The rain finally decides –

"I can't come to spoil the view from this window,
let the view from this window stay luminated.
Hail! This special window and hats off to the magical
view created!

The Fantasy World

I feel happy and secure in my own world of fantasy,
please keep reality away from me.
Throughout, the fantasy world has been the grip; it held me tight and not let me trip.

It's been easing the tension and soothing the pain.
Only for the sake of fantasy world, I escaped reality again and again.
Therefore calm I still remain.

The Fantasy world is satisfactory, gives some energy to connect back with the soul. It's the main source, to carry on with the life goal.
This fantasy world is very precious to me, beyond words to explain the feel ...
I'm glad it's only mine and no one can steal.

It would have been really nice,
if the Fantasy World was real.

Why Do I Keep Writing?

By putting pen to paper again and again. Writing becomes a necessity, a passion to claim.

I'm incomplete without writing, like a pendant without its chain.
Writing symbolises my happiness only words can explain!

It's my key to positivity, opening the inner door, just with the splash of some ink – I'm entitled to explore!

Being kindled with the power of writing, I can rise up sky-high.
Flying away with soulful words, with meanings that cannot lie.

When a writer, writes righteously, even the real can merge with fantasy.

How can I not dream while writing?

How can I not create something exciting?

The blank page gives me a right to dream, picturising an imagery which is totally unseen –
Imagination rules the world ... where any kind of adventure is held.

When I embrace my two close friends paper and pen, we form magic of miracles to awaken again and again!

Writing is more than just language and punctuation:
It's a platform where you can master – a world of your own creation ...

When the Brain Had a Chat With the Heart!

Brain: 'Oh mysterious heart, why are you always the centre of attention? I should be the only subject, every human should mention!'

Heart: 'Oh my friend brain, how should I explain? Listen to me carefully, unreasonable is your complain! We are both weapons to the human, we both have an aim. It's impossible to work without each other, for one to play the life game.'

Brain: 'What's the difference between you and me?'

Heart: 'When you get heated up as fire, I remain cool like the sea. That's the type of difference between you and me.

'You are rational, very powerful and smart. However, I live with devotion and emotion, I'm the innocent part.

'You're the horse and I'm your rider

You're the thought and I'm your inspirer
You're the flower, I'm your fragrance
You're the sun and I'm your radiance.

'When it's hard for you to choose, I decide. When you're losing track, I'm there to guide. We both work together and are incomplete – without each other.'

Brain: 'Conquer the mind, conquer the world – I hear the humans say.'

Heart: 'Always listen to the inner voice of your heart, they also do convey.'

Brain: 'Please clarify to me your riddles, what are you exactly trying to say?'

Heart: 'You're an ocean of thoughts, running all over the place. That's why the humans want to conquer you, to keep you into one place.

'However, I'm peaceful and static, unlike you rushing here and there. Spirituality is my dominance; it's pure energy which cannot disappear.

'When my celestial vibes connect to you, all humans feel positive and let go of stress.

'I believe if we both happily work together, humans can resolve the rest!'

Brain: 'Thank you Heart for awakening me with the goodness of knowledge. Today I feel blessed.'

Hope this chat gave answers to anyone confused. All the best!

Why Be Too Judgemental?

Why be too judgemental, have you never made a mistake?

Why be too judgemental, are you built-in truthful without a pinch of fake?

Why be too judgemental, are you completely transparent and have never been opaque?

Why be too judgemental, are you above the prime creator's jury?

Why be too judgemental, are you the owner of forgiveness and fury?

Why be too judgemental, are you 24/7 filter-free?

Why be too judgemental when we all have flaws and that's reality ...

Let's not be too judgemental, imperfections are bound to be.

It's part of being human – just like you and me ...

Today the Wardrobe Was Talking to Me ...

The cap that I was wearing, began with a sentence very new:
'You will do something tremendous today, therefore my "hat's off" to you.'

An eyelash hair dropped on my cheek, hoping all my wishes come true.

My secret perfume was promising today,
for it to last a longer way.

As I was wearing my pair of earrings, a whisper for me they were preparing:
'You will shine like a star, so forget the fearing.'
That's the different types of things – I was hearing.

Today the blush of my cheeks complained:
'Just stop it now, we've had enough of you shying.'

Today my favourite ring requested: 'Just put me on, I'm worth your trying.'

Today I wore a smart watch that said:
'This time shall be in your favour, waiting through the day.'

Today I wore a chain around my neck that said:
'The finest version of you is yet to unveil, embrace the day and have the feel.'

Today I devoted a token of trust to God,
just before I was leaving the door:
'I'm always with you,' he indicated towards me. It's only then when I felt sure.

Today I wore the most protective shoes, which will comfort all the pathway.

Today I put on my biggest rucksack that said:
'You will bag it home with happiness coming to stay.'

Finally, even the mirror praised my reflection by saying:
'You have dressed your best today.'

A Heart the Secret Place ...

A heart is a briefcase full of secrets, a personal locker with the untold story.

A heart of gold beats with glory.

It's only the owner who can access the heart; it's an unseen private place.

No one else has the password to log in for information; it's a full-on secured space.

A heart is tightly wrapped inside, floating with an ocean of mystery.
Keeping notes of past, present and the future coming history.

A heart is blessed with a powerful shield, protecting any content being revealed!

A matter which is not to mention, that doesn't need too much attention, may quietly sit inside this heart, by keeping tension and stress apart.

Safely each subject in detail has entitlement to rule – residing in this heart.

Relaxed they all can stay, covering the weirdest stuff away – things that the lips and tongue wouldn't dare to convey!

Very mighty and strong is this little organ heart, where such heavy material is hidden so smart!

Eyes

These eyes have so much to say; we see them talk, every day.

A thousand words, one eye can convey.

These eyes will speak, what the mouth cannot say.

When we want second opinion, we always glance into those eyes, as we know they struggle with lies.

These eyes are a window to dreams; we can get lost in the glare – with just a single stare.

So next time be careful when you look in there – you must be aware ...

These eyes are universal and enchanting, full of desire waiting and demanding.

If these eyes have a potential goal, they can actually arrow any heart or soul ...

These eyes in particular, play the biggest role!

LIFE IN A LOCKDOWN!

The pandemic arrived with an unwelcomed, shocking wave.
Everyone got confused and didn't know how to behave!
It targeted both the smart and naive.

The 'sanitising gel' became a household name, a hygiene freak – everyone became!
Keeping fit and healthy was the main aim.

This lockdown came with bundles of stress, the toughest time –
the 'nature's test'.
Where everyone got tired with loads of 'rest', waiting for a hint to go out was a matter of big interest!

Even the most glamourous individuals were 'deadly dressed' at home.
Putting the make-up kit aside, tackling stress alone.

Saving food and drink was a serious matter to think, with several times of hand-washing – a 'family queue' beside the sink!

However, for some this lockdown was a self-evolving phase, picking up the pieces, making sense – by putting some things back into place.

The silence was deep and peaceful for understanding the soul.
Reflecting on life and setting new goals.
This lockdown brought immense new change,
life is different now – a feeling that's strange!

Life After Lockdown

Picking up the pieces, gathered after then.
Life is confusing now, a lot different to back then ...
The news is like sipping a bitter potion, adding hints of sugar each time – just hoping now, it all stays fine.

Some now value this new shape of life a lot more,

whereas some mind frames are reluctant, to even leave the door.

The new norm has now taken a central lead,
masks and gloves forming the new 'not well' looks,
making it hard to breathe.

Normality is a desire now, which we all want to retrieve,

It's a global change impacting the world, very hard to believe.

By caring for each other we surely can succeed.

Good Time Will Come ...

Good time will come for everyone,

meanwhile, cherish the memories when it was fun.

Life always brings up punches and twists,

but not for long, can they stay on our wrists.

Very soon – they will be dismissed.

Stay bright in every colour and shade,

don't give permission for hope to fade.

You mustn't let negativity invade.

Upgrade your dream even more,

don't let your belief degrade.

Let faith be the motivation and success be your trade.

Nostalgic College

It was fun in college, it topped us with knowledge!

Had fun following some of the fashion trends, even though recalling them now – sweetly offends!

That time was simple, with an innocent theme.
Jingle bells everywhere with a melodious team.

Every Monday was a special treat; Sam's spicy chips us friends used to eat. Straight after that was internet time, in the learning waves centre – with a close friend of mine. Before the study session started, we made most of the break, a glimpse of favourite serials, rushing to our computers, we did have to take!

Doing presentable work was always my mega-aim.

"Lucky you strive for perfection," was my tutor's claim!

Passing the diploma, became the 'talk of the town'.

It was like receiving a winner's crown!

Thankfully got across the challenges, passing all the tests.

Hail! that college in East Ham, for me it was the best!

A special thank you to those sincere teachers, who gave us the wisdom to educate and celebrate.

That experience was like a surprise gift given to me. The most wonderful things happened, the best that could be!

A fabulous journey of study and friends, together they made the perfect blend. It was a mesmerising time, that will always make me bow,

mind-blowing, just wow!

Simplicity

There is beauty in simplicity,

a practice which can make life pretty.
Simplicity signifies sophistication,

allows easy flow without complication.
It's a notion of belief,
with raw imagination.
When it's simple, it's filter-free,
a taste from originality.

Camera flashes are not always needed,
or else the painter wouldn't have succeeded.
An embellished fancy card, may be eye-catchy,
but a handwritten note of love – is a lot more 'touchy'.

A lipstick colour may last a while,
but nothing can beat the power of a smile.

www.marciampublishing.com

www.ingramcontent.com/pod-product-compliance
Lightning Source LLC
Chambersburg PA
CBHW070341120526
44590CB00017B/2970